Purchased at N.S.P.C.C. bazaar - Claridges Hotel
26-11-1979

TED WALKER

The Night Bathers

Poems 1966-8

Jonathan Cape Thirty Bedford Square London

First published 1970
© 1970 by Ted Walker

Jonathan Cape Ltd, 30 Bedford Square, London, wc1

s b n 224 61808 3

Printed and bound in Great Britain by
Richard Clay (The Chaucer Press) Ltd, Bungay Suffolk

Contents

Note

In this collection I have included
some translations from French, German,
Spanish and Italian poems. Rather
than put them in a separate section of
the book, I have preferred to have
them among my own poems, where they
seem to provide a continuity of
theme or mood.

    I am indebted to all my friends, above
all to Leslie Norris, for help, advice
and encouragement.

T.W.

Acknowledgments

The poems 'Sunday drive to the beach', 'The harpooning', 'The pythons', 'Grass', 'Journey back', 'A place of trees' and 'Swallows' appeared originally in the *New Yorker* (© 1967, 1968 and 1969, The New Yorker Magazine, Inc.). Thanks are also due to the B.B.C. Third Programme, the *London Magazine*, the *New York Times*, the *Poetry Review*, *Priapus*, the *Sunday Telegraph*, the *Journals of Pierre Menard* and the *Sunday Times*.

FOR MY FRIENDS

THE NIGHT BATHERS

For John Charles Walker,
killed on Shoreham beach

I don't think you would ever have approved
Of being in a poem. 'Mushty, look,'
I hear your spectre saying, 'keep it dark;
I wouldn't want my mates to get to know.'
But, uncle, how else can I honour you?
Time's gone when I could do the things you did.

At Cambridge I came close to what you were,
Being choked by intellectual simoom;
My most cerebral action there was the soft-
Selling of advert space in *Cambridge Left*
To the boss of a fish-and-chip saloon.
Literally, I wore the coat you wore —

The jacket of that white alpaca suit
You dared the yobs to jeer on Worthing Prom.
My pals all wondered where I'd nicked it from
And, Brando-esque in leather, named a hand
In Poker after me. Two of a kind
I think we were in the days of that coat.

On pay-days in the shipyard you played Brag
Around an oil-drum with a greasy pack
A week's wages slipped through. You'd borrow back
Enough to stand a round of beer later.
Down The Marlipins they say you were
The sort that got offered a man's last fag.

That was before the war. Sometimes your ghost
Enters my mind, dressed in some comical
Garb; aptly in white, on a bicycle,
Fresh from a battle with lime-bags; or wet
After a fifty-foot plunge for a bet
At midnight in the Adur. It was just

Your luck to get away with it. And when
I get most sick of my gentility
And all my careful life's futility —
Pruning the bloody roses for next year,
Setting the prunings tidily on fire,
Sweeping the ashes away – why, it's then

I almost envy you that booby-trap.
All alive-o you strolled to pinch firewood
From the one innocent house that still stood
On Shoreham beach. *You* never knew what it meant
To look for blood in your daily excrement;
You never knew the mine that blew you up.

Washing the body (after Rilke)

By now they were used to him. But
when the kitchen lamp was brought,

fitfully burning in a dark draught,
the Stranger was alien. His throat

they swabbed. Not knowing his past,
they lied him a life as they washed.

One of them stopped and coughed.
The heavy, vinegar sponge she left

on his face. Through the silence
the woman with her, too, had to pause.

The stiff brush let its drops tap.

Grisly, his cramped hand tried to announce
his lack of thirst throughout the house.

And did. Coughing, they resumed.
Self-consciously, more hurried,

they resumed. While, on the papered
wall, twisting, wallowing, crooked,

their shadows swam trapped in a net
till the washing was complete.

In the window, curtainless,
was brutal night. One, nameless,

lay there, clean, bare, issuing laws.

Insomniac

Walk behind night, too tired for sleep,
Through buckthorn ill of the moon.
Sea heaves in a puckered hide, thrown elephant.
Barley fields lap, and oats, awash with poppies.
Unmoor, unmoor, my arms; rehearse
Rowing to open water. Shipped oars
Would warm with salt, rough
In a sun adrift where nothing is sung.

Birth of a merman

(for Kit Barker)

After the visiting waterbird had done,
Sea slid in along the final oil
And again
He knew unmillioning every cell
Of tissue under the man-skull.

All this had happened to him before,
His immemorial bodies. Once more
The soft squab
Belly was split to the fingering crab,
And bones sank slow to the ocean floor,

And it was finished, the human death.
By first morning water-light he rose
To burst in froth,
Astonishing white, spontaneous
Surf upon stillness. On the warmth

Of drifting foam rushed engender-
ing air to riffle him in the sun.
The slender
Edge of him lay for the dark when
Lightning would strike and thunder

Drop crammed power. A wave-back
Gathered into ribs, tautened the black
Weed that was skin,
Wind its knitting unguent. In
One scissoring minute he was made. Rain

Hissed awash. He felt. He was webbed.
The raw, sudden lungs accepted breath.
The grey, dabbed
Sands were astir with him. He rubbed
The weatherless corridors, searching for earth.

The harpooning

Where the seas are open moor
and level blue, limitless,
and swells are as soft grasses
rolling over with the wind,
often to the idleness
of Azorean summer

come the great whales. Long granite
grow, slowly awash with sun,
and waves lap along black skin
like the shine of a laving
rain upon a city pavement.
Together they come, yet alone

they seem to lie. Massively
still, they bask, breathing like men.
Silent among them there is one
so huge he enters the eye
whole, leaving the rest unseen.
His sons and his cows idly

loll, as if in wait. Inside
him, too, tethered now, there waits
the bulk and strength of a herd
of a dozen rogue elephant;
they strain taut thongs of his will,
and paw against such indolence.

Anger could snap them loose—
anger, or hunger. Jungles
under a mile of ocean,
where no light has ever been,
would splinter, and the blind squid
uncoil in him like oily trees.

But the squint jaws close on bone
steady as a castle door-jamb;
and, bigger than a drawbridge,
his tail flukes are calm upon
the calmer water. While the sun
still pleases him, he will grudge

himself no pleasure. He blows
old air from his old lungs, cones
rising whitely. Through the hard,
final coursings of his blood
the oars will not rouse him. Thick
blubber houses him like hot meringue.

The pythons

(for Tom Maschler)

Deep in caves under Java,
white snakes with purposeless eyes
live by the plain behaviour

of fanging at any noise
not of water dropped on rock.
Scuttering among runways,

they listen for where to look,
swallow, and dream a sleep of tastes;
are deaf of the want of dark

when a gatherer's lamp infests
their corridor. While poles probe
the musting, edible nests

spittled by swifts, one swung club
of light is enough to stun
lissomness stiff to a tube.

It's then the lazar-house stone
in the colourless, still pit
moves, beginning to be green

and living for being lit.
Nests stack, like clutches of skulls
in a catacomb, or split,

spilling dust the blackness pulls.
Deliberate, entranced like
a visionary, the boy fills

sacks with what he came to seek,
safe within his proven cone
of brilliance; then comes back

on a swing of rope, alone.
And, knowing the white ears stare
out of glidings that begin

under his shadow once more,
he climbs to surface slowly
through deep terraces of prayer,

holding the pythons holy.

Grass

Whoever has travelled in grassless places
Remembers for ever the upward stare
Of blind earth eying out of pits
To gaze
A skull-face changeless over the bone.

I am thankful for the grass I own.
It clothes bare tilth that my
Deliberate seed refuses;
It grafts an
Unbidden skin over the permanent soil.

But I have known it fail:
Given as the snow, it is taken away
In arid summers. When evenings grow
Ungardenly
With broadcasts of oriental war,

I have stood at my open door
Remembering the wild rice of Asia
Teeming in waste, unpeopled swamps,
And the blanched
Lepers corroding through the cities.

Near them, where no grass is,
The slat-flanked cattle sometimes come,
Bringing a shrivelled cud gathered
From far off.
Rare seed falls on them from long-flighted birds.

Moon ashes

For longer than time is left me,
Breast-high among the ashes I swam.
While there was earth-light to travel by,
I knew behind their white, soft,
Terrible collapse upon themselves
And how they evened over where I had come
Like windless waters levelling after a skiff.

The dark came, easier. I guess
What silent myriads will fall
Upward from my path, beginnings of snow,
As though this were Earth. Fierce
For hard, high ground where no fleck settles,
I shoulder away from the crater's centre,
Carrying no flag, no token crucifix.

The heart of Hialmar
(after Leconte de Lisle)

Icy wind, crystal night. The snow is red.
Countless warriors sleep under the stars,
Haggard-eyed, sword in hand. Not one moves. Caws
Of black ravens rasp the air overhead.

Cold flames of moonlight lick far and wide.
Among the mangled corpses Hialmar
Rises, both hands heavy on his sword-bar;
Blood gushes crimson from his wounded side.

He cries, 'Is there left even one to cling
To life, of all those lusty youths that sang
This morning when their happy voices rang
As stridently as thicket blackbirds sing?

Dumb. My helmet's smashed. My armour hangs free,
Holed by the battle-axe, the studs all sprung.
My eyes bleed, and I hear a dirge that's sung
Like wolf-howls or the moaning of the sea.

Come, bold raven, eating men is thy art,
Pick my breast open with thy iron beak;
Such as we are, tomorrow, come and seek.
To Ylmer's daughter carry my warm heart.

To Uppsala, where the Jarls drink honest beer
And sing with golden goblets in their fists,
Fly swiftly there, O prowler of the mists,
And carry thou my heart to her that's dear.

At a tower-top where the jackdaws fly
She will be standing, white, with long black hair;
Two rings of finest silver she will wear,
Her eyes are brighter than the summer sky.

Go, dark messenger, tell her my love's true
And that I send my heart that she may know
That it is red and strong, not frail and slow;
Ylmer's daughter, raven, will smile for you.

My soul pours out from twenty wounds. Life's done.
I've had my time; wolves, drink this crimson flood.
Young, courageous, laughing, free, pure my blood,
With the gods I take my place in the sun.'

Snow asthma

Sifting into silence
　　Until the yard was filled,
Snow was a sudden comer
　　When I was a child.

Bullfinches were in bloom
　　On a bough of dead apple;
As though the moon made daylight,
　　Shadow was purple.

Seldom as bereavement
　　Came snow. For a brief
Morning my mother's face
　　Looked underlit with grief.

She threw ashes on the path
　　And dug out the gate;
She kept watch along the road
　　Until it grew late.

Whatever was to come
　　That time kept away,
But through my window's wide-awake
　　And sunken eye

I stared from my smother
　　While unmolestable snow
Thick on a conifer-top
　　Stifled its crow.

Thaw

A cooling sudden
as snowfall by night
made love's earth harden;

with crystals of hate
winter had trodden
our solitude tight.

Then we were broken
for once in a way;
we were turned to the sun

and our frost was taken
like double-dug clay
whose shives fall open

Journey back

Uncertain day in certain
winter. The Midland counties
clodded in November's ruck.
At mid-morning's latent dark,
air the violet of rubbed eyes,
it looks too late to begin

back. After a dozen miles
of wharf, slate roof on the sag,
I glimpse a gruel of hills
past railed Victorian schools, black
terrace-ends, metallic slag,
and feast on a broken oak

harbouring crows. Looping wires
lead, full of silent voices,
home, southward out. If I spoke
to my family now, heard noises
of their playing, like fires
crackling live in the kiosk,

I'd warm no more than the least
acre of this loneliness;
vastly its landscape swims, lost
beyond its minor byroads —
land without finish. I press
on, making my diamonds

in the tilth of the year's first
snow. Headlamps winnow its chaff;
the windscreen packs with mooncrust.
London, Surrey and the Weald
hush under me. Close enough
now to a recognized cold —

this line of poplars I know,
branches cordoned like police –
guiltily I stop with less
than ten easy miles to go
and dial my number. My voice
seems confident as it says,

It's good to be coming home,
look forward to seeing you,
having a practised cadence,
habitual, therefore true.
And as the last turnings come
through the hanger wood, I sense

a relief in familiar
landscapes of a solitude
rooted here: that will be known
season and season beyond
this night, this cold, these thrown
regattas of foundered snow.

A place of trees

(for Bernard Price)

They've been felling. From the copse
Beside the lane, all day long,
I have listened to the collapse
Of timber, the mad saw wailing

Agonized while it spun free,
And then the blade's grateful moan
As it cracked another tree
Like a dog splintering a bone.

Thinking I'd take a last look,
I came when the men had left.
In the failing light the smoke
Of their bonfires lingered soft

Among the wilting laurels
That used to grow in the dark.
The raw stumps were tar-barrels
Open to the shooting spark,

But by those flares I could recall
No individual trunk,
No limb, or any single
Leaf of what lived here. I think

In this winter night only
Of close, high-summer shadows
Gathering over a lonely
Visitor. A dirt path shows

The way he came to this place
Of trees. It leads into a dry
Field, and fields beyond, then space
Beyond the last star of the sky.

Hothouse

There was a place in his mind
where the man could be alone
from choice, free from his children
and not at home to his friend;
where husband was husbandman

not to be called to his food
but in his own time. He made
all weather that entered; took
rain from a pipe at the flood
or trickle, as the mood took

him. He could put out the sun
with lime-wash over the glass,
could waft on his leaves cool airs
at will. He saw a season
breed that was not the summer's,

all summer. He was a god
come to crucify his trees
on wires. Whatever would grow
would grow as he thought was good.
In winter he lit his fires

covertly in a furnace-house:
new stars to warm his planet.
Lamps left to burn through midnight
lit the sliding snow-waters
from the roof. He would delight

in visiting his blossom,
come spring, with a rabbit's scut.
Before the first bees were out,

busily his hands would swarm;
infallible crops would set.

When he bruised the ripened fruit,
he savoured an urgent juice
that spilled in his hand. The house
had swollen more than he could eat.
Nectarines were everyone's.

In an hour they'd pick him bare
and leave goodbyes. He would stay
a little while, after. He
would be tired at the door
where the strange day-lilies sway.

Hillpath

Soft for the sun
as no stone
for footfall deaf

hot chalk I
trod through the
moth noon led

to thick sprucewood
floors listening
for conefall

Stone

Too tired, after, even to close my eyes,
In the half-dark I saw her skin for stone,
So motionless. I waited for the rise
Or falling of her breast, but there came none:
She seemed too tired, after, even to breathe,

And does not feel these lizard fingers writhe
Over her now. I'll let my lids half close
And bask till the last of her warmth has gone
And the morning's entering cloudlight shows
Her stone for flesh, my flesh for stone again.

Bring me a sunflower...
(after Montale)

Bring me a sunflower to plant in my earth
Burnt with sea-salt;
Let me turn its face of yellow anxiety
All day to the sky's mirrored blues:

For dark things aspire to the bright,
Bodies are consumed in floods of shade
And these consumed in music.
To vanish is the ultimate of luck.

So bring me the plant that will lead me
There, where the sun's depth rises,
And life is a spirit-vapour lifting.
Bring me the sunflower crazed with light.

Dewdrop

Blue in a lupin-leaf
after-dawn diamond
unliquidly
shone

A simple brilliant
eating the face
of the morning
sun

A crystal of night as
hard as star-glint
fixed as owl-
eye

Closing upon some inner
darkness tinily
it mirrored
me

Swallows

A day of winter-slaked April.
Bobbers on a wire at a wall –
trindles of fire-blued iron
that any wind twitches – twirl
and are lifted into swallows.

Little particles of thirst,
the red of summer brickdust
are those throats among a month
avaricious of its damp; fust
of the whitening lichen,

buffed by delicate bellies,
comes live out of its ice.
Blue is warm of swallows' wings:
rich spillings of their sapphires
glint along the dark, nettled end

of garden. They are my claim –
over half a world they come,
crop-full of Africa, to lodge
in crevices of my home.
In honorance of such plenty,

I make them a plot of hotness
to skim upon: hibiscus,
hyssop, pools of buddleia,
a humming of mulberries.
I fork the brown mulch of one

summer less into my earth
as warm weather falls. Noth-
ing can encourage their coming
again. I leave them be, with
an untouched, vulnerable clutch

of another year's small flesh.
Soon my eyes must relinquish
them. When the hips are redder
than the roses were, they'll brush
my willow a final time,

flying out of the house.
And, a continent deep, I sense
some other self – between us,
paltry, diminishing oceans
and arid, vanishing land.

Kraaled in a vast and untreed
veld, his sleep is troubled.
My wall of lichen relapses white.
In the night he lifts his head,
listening for ultimate swallows.

The sleep of apples (after Lorca)

I long to sleep the sleep of apples, far
from the blast of graveyards,
sleep the sleep of the boy who tried
to cut his heart out over the sea.

Tell me no more the dead can't bleed,
that the rotted mouth still asks for water.
The atrocities of grass,
the snake-jawed moon
that chews before dawn –
no concern of mine.

A little while I want
to sleep, a little while, a
minute, a century.
But let
everybody know: I have not died;
the golden stable is at my lips,
I am the west wind's crony,
I, the vastest shadow of my teardrops.

Come daybreak, pull the sheet over me
from the dawn's flung fistful of ants;
use hard water to wet my shoes,
to make the first light's scorpion-pincers slip.

For I long for the sleep of apples, and
to learn some song to purge me of earth;
long to be beside the solemn child
who tried to cut his heart out over the sea.

Elderberries

Every night I would pass the elderberries
Severally aglimmer from a composite eye
Sunk in the dark of leaves that desolately
Stank to the village lamplight. Memories

Of elders past I gathered, those within reach,
Picking at will. Almost, I could almost touch
The thick inflorescences of autumn stars
That colder air remembered of the elders,

So soon after summer. Skies brimmed a taut pool
Of known patterning. I searched for the blossom
To drop from some forgotten tree, but random
Petals drowned evanescently. Beyond recall,

Whatever it was that had been terrible,
Once. Elders, elders: I had by heart the smell,
And it had to do with loneliness – often,
Hot from the stare of an unfrequented lane,

I'd snatched off a hollow stem to dig my nail
Hard and deep into the white, the secret pith.
But it wasn't this. Something else I had with
Me, out in the empty street. I'd pass my wall

Encrusted with pygmy, indigo mirrors
Night after night, wondering; step out of doors
Straight into them, into the berries, and slide
Fast from the lamplight edging their unlit side.

The ghost of Dafydd ap Gwilym (fl 1340-70) at a drowned valley reservoir

I went from a lusher country than
This. I wander through hollow pastures
Of stone, scrabbling up the bare sheep-runs,
Looking for warmer grass to lie in;

Somewhere it must grow, in the summer
Of this upland place. I want comfort
Such as crimson whinberries will not
Offer. Once, far below, the glimmer

Of winds moved like veined liquid among
The dank meadows of a thigh-deep farm;
There was a gasping torrent to swim
Before love, and after love. I long

For the vanished house, and the shadow
I knew before this shivering sunshine,
Long for every quibbling girl I've lain
With in unfenced Wales. I recall how

Afterwards and alone I would climb
To see the buzzard's silent hook fall
Plumb to a tuft at the lip of the hill
Where slim leverets had slipped from their dam

In their wet fur momently. There are
Square, blank forests of alien trees
Here now, growing in orderly rows
Where silver birches raggedly were:

But whether there are thrushes to sing
In them I would not guess; nor whether

One snatch of passion is left that the
Bards and thrushes of my time headlong

Clamoured to the carolling valleys.
I listen for some voice to answer
Mine across this flat, ineloquent water;
Voices of girls calling to shrill boys,

Men's voices with soft-speaking women.
Is no lilting syllable of love
Still whispered here, where a man could live
By the old wisdoms of the tavern?

Duw Mawr, once in this deep valley bed
From a girl's mouth I drank philosophy!
I listen: if I hear words, away
In the wind they are words from the dead.

I was beckoned by a wan harlot,
Yet returned, like many a Welshman,
To the arms of my country. Again
I see her face of rock, sky, water; but

Among her ruin, her fallen walls,
I move in search of her memory
Back to the tomb in a skeletal Abbey,
Under the remembered grass of Wales.

The night bathers

I walk, a stranger here,
in alien, emptying Wales
through orange montbretia
wild among fallen walls
of a left, profitless farm
where only visitors come.

Along the promontory
warm of an indolent lick
Of August water, hazes
close on a momentary crow.
Dark is a lenient harm
over Cardiganshire.

I am alone as now
my son is alone. Below
the headland he worries at sleep
where bushes breathe the evening
in. Troubles of honeysuckle
film his air. Remorse of mine

wrapped him about too warm;
he wrestled off my comforting.
A thunder sensed in other hills
has moved away. Rain would ease him
but it will not rain. All day,
as sands of little birds lifted

in a strapping summer wind
that smacked canvas brittle with sun,
I was aware of health and
used it bitterly in play,
pitiless against the man
growing from the sullen boy

rid of me now. I made him
run out the slack of the tide
till sand was dry on his tiredness
and the sea was a far, shut bud.
Now, as he ebbs in a dream
from the pull of my contrition,

I hear the night bathers come
over the yelping stones. I see
by astonishing bonfires
in an idleness of yachts
my father running down the beach
twenty grown years ago, at home;

when he was young to understand
why, momently out of the night
and purposeful beyond the reach
of all his worry, I had swum
deep into banks of sea-fret
too far to have to answer him.

Bonfire

Final nightfall of summer.
I scrape a match at the wall,
cup safe the flame. Cracked hands smell
of earth and ripening pear
that I breathe, beginning fire.

All afternoon was the waft
from blue fields, the stubble-scorch,
pricking me to this. I crouch
like an ancient to my craft,
knowing this moment to lift

dry leafage to little twigs
and lean to a locked apex
the slats of a smashed apple-box.
Gripping broken ladder-legs,
the blaze skips up to long logs

of old, wasp-ruddled fruitwood.
I rub with a rough stick spark-
showers down, petals from the bark,
and listen for the first, hard
apricot fireball to thud

dull among the underheat.
And it is done, my pleasure.
I smother the sprinting fire
with swaths of nettles I swapped
an hour since, failed dahlias ripped

from faded ceremony,
and pulped, unflowered irises.
I watch as the smoke rises,

inclining slow towards my
house, and upwards, and away,

then leave my fire in darkness.
Indoors, with every window
tight, I start to feel the glow
of nettle-throb on my face,
and sit with smoke's bitterness

steeped in my clothes. My closed eyes
remember a settling gleed,
white, red, clinking. Outside,
where the last of summer burns,
my soil lies clean for the ice.

Middle-age (after Hölderlin)

Over the lake there hangs
a land of yellow pears
and rife with dog-roses

You perfect swans
tipsy with kisses
dipping your heads
in the probity
of holy water

Wherever when winter
comes ah where shall I
find flowers and sunshine
and shadows of the land?

Imminent walls cold
without words

In the wind
rattle the weathercocks

Mary's carol (after Lope de Vega)

Holy angels in the palms,
hold your branches still
while my baby is asleep;

O palm trees of Bethlehem
tossed in the angry winds,
make no sound for Him

while my baby is asleep,
but hold your branches still.
God's little boy is tired

with weeping – let Him rest
from His mild tears now;
hold your branches still

while my baby is asleep.
The rock frosts about Him
and He has no coverlet;

holy angels of the trees,
hold your branches still
so my little child may sleep.

Joseph speaks to the midwife of Bethlehem

You made me wait outside the stable door.
You had your work to do. Nobody knew
It was the Son of God my Mary bore.

In Bethlehem the winter nights are raw;
But while the wind from Hebron's summit blew,
You made me wait outside. The stable door

Was sealed with frost. I made a fire and saw
The cattle restless when the cinders flew.
It was the Son of God my Mary bore

That night, beside the manger, on the floor,
Frightened and cold. Little though I could do,
You made me wait. Outside the stable door

You called to me, told me to gather straw
For Him to lie upon. A baby Jew
It was – the Son of God my Mary bore

Had looks like mine. And in His face I saw
This light that I forgive you by: for though
You made me wait outside the stable door,
It *was* the Son of God my Mary bore.

February poem

The hours of daylight must be lengthening now:
I walked among the frost and noticed how
The last, softening snowdrops were in thaw;
Then, stepping between flecks of shadow, saw
The first collapse of crocuses begun,
Yellowy in small fritterings of sun.
Ridiculous with delight, I hurried home.

But I stare from a winter-facing room
To think how premature the petal-fall
Of laurustinus by the churchyard wall;
And as the minutes edge me from the light
Into this perceptibly shorter night,
I sense a northerly gathering of air
Prising another bud of my despair.

To the Fates (after Hölderlin)

Just one more summer grant to me, Mighty Ones!
And, that my song may ripen, one autumn more;
My heart more gladly could expire then,
Surfeited utterly with my music.

No soul secures its god-given right in life
And neither finds in Orcus hereafter rest;
But, once I have achieved my sacred
Object, the poem my heart now yearns for,

O welcome then, repose of the phantom world!
Contentment I shall find, though without my lyre
To guide my footsteps onward; only
Once to live god-like, no more is needed.